THEOLOGY *of* HOME III

Cover and Layout Design: Caroline Green, David Ferris, Scribe Inc.
Photography and Cover image: Kim Baile. Stella Maris image © Lauren Gulde, Santa Clara Designs. Japanese Sea Wave, Pannawish, Shutterstock. Used with permission.
Location: Special thanks to Tiffany Caliva, owner of the "The Beach Lodge", Oxnard, CA.

ISBN: 978-1-5051-2293-0
Kindle ISBN: 978-1-5051-2294-7
ePub ISBN: 978-1-5051-2295-4

Published in the United States by
TAN Books
PO Box 269
Gastonia, NC 28053
www.TANBooks.com

Printed in the United States of America

THEOLOGY *of* HOME III

At the Sea

CARRIE GRESS

NOELLE MERING

Photography KIM BAILE

TAN Books

Gastonia, North Carolina

To
Hazel Karin Maria Baile
(1935–2021)

With deep gratitude for your life
and all you brought
to Theology of Home

Contents

Authors' Note

Since the subject of home is so personal, it was only natural for us to include personal stories from our lives as wives and mothers. But as the nature of co-authorship dictates, you don't always know who is speaking. Part of the beauty of this book is the universal theme of home, and as such, our personal stories are meant to convey deeper truths, making the actual owner of our individual stories not nearly as important as the message the story conveys. We hope this does not distract from your reading of the text.

Introduction

It starts with a most basic element: water.

One drop at a time.

"Water," Leonardo da Vinci observed, "is the driving force of all nature." All day long, we wipe, rinse, wash, soak, sip, douse, spray, pour, quench, splash, and sprinkle it. We scarcely give attention to its importance until we are faced with its absence or its enormity in the vast expanse of the sea.

The sea is man's first playground. We have flocked to it in droves for sustenance, recreation, vacation, restoration, and relaxation. The steady pounding of the waves holds our attention, delights us as we splash in its surf, and lulls us to sleep when we close our eyes. Life at the sea is so commonplace that references to it pepper our language in ways we scarcely consider; everyday words like *navigate, inundate, flood, flounder, ebb and flow, sail,* and *buoy.*

It is no accident that high cliffs and bluffs are prime real estate. Whether on a pristine day or accompanied by the unfolding drama of wind and clouds, light and dark, we are mesmerized. A sea view was the first theatre. The founders of Venice loved it all so much that they perched their city directly upon the very sea itself.

Of course, there is also a dark side to the sea. It is unfathomably big, unpredictable, untamable, and unrelenting. Even that fluid boundary where land meets water shifts as the years pass. Little is left untouched by the erosion of tides and the spray of salt water, the battering of the surf or the weight of wind.

"No literature is richer than that of the sea.
No story is more enthralling,
no tradition is more secure."

—FELIX RIESENBERG

Epic tales like *The Odyssey*, *Moby Dick*, and the *Master and Commander* series and the explorations of the likes of Columbus, Drake, and Magellan have enchanted us since the dawn of history. In these stories of adventure and woe, the human spirit and the great drama of life, the sea becomes setting, symbol, and character, imbuing the entirety of the story and the psyches of the subjects.

This double nature of light and dark leaves us a bit off balance. The sea is a source of innocent delight for children, treated with the lightness of a

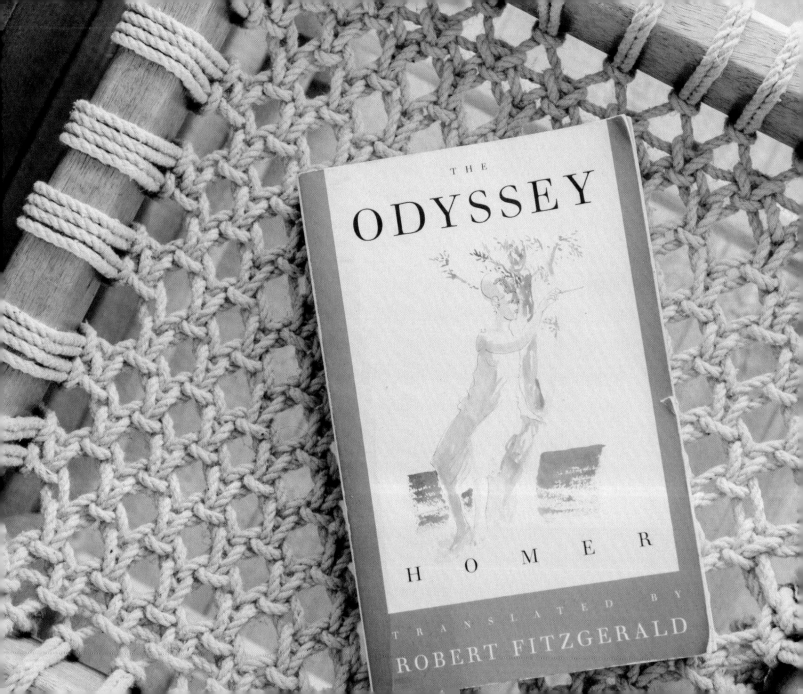

Women on the Shore

There is a distinct pattern to the sea throughout history and cultures; more often than not, women are the ones left behind as men set sail for war, wares, food, or trade. There are many reasons for it, but seemingly the most obvious is that ships are tough places to live, especially when engaged in warfare. Women were also needed to tend children and a home, farm, or family business. Ships and ports are also home to unsavory individuals that no sane man would want engaging with his wife and children.

Perhaps the most famous among the waiting women is Penelope, the wife of Odysseus, who waited "twenty wearisome years" for her husband to return. The quick-witted Penelope fought off suitors with various tactics, including the agreement that she would marry when she had finished weaving a burial shroud for her father-in-law. By day, she would weave, but by night, she would unravel the day's work.

But then, as if in a dream, Odysseus finally does come home. His arrival was not as one would expect; he came in disguise as a common beggar to avenge those who had tried to marry his wife and frittered away his estate.

Penelope's maid breaks the news first.

> "Wake up Penelope, dear child, and see with your very own eyes what you've longed for all these days. Odysseus has come and is *home* after all these years."
>
> Penelope's heart leapt up. She sprang from the bed and clung to the old woman, and the tears streaming from her eyes, and spoke winged words. "Dear nurse, I beg you for the truth! If he is really home, as you say, how on earth did he single-handed overcome those shameless suitors who were always hanging about the house in a pack?"

Not quite believing her eyes, for it had been twenty long years, Penelope puts her husband-in-disguise to a test. She asks her slave to move the bed in their bridal chamber, but Odysseus protests, reminding her that it cannot be moved, for he made the bed himself, and so he knows that one of the posts is made of a living olive tree. With that, Penelope knows that he is her husband, and the words of their reunion have echoed through history.

> Her words stirred a great longing for tears in Odysseus' heart, and he wept as he held his dear and loyal wife in his arms. It was like the moment when the blissful land is seen by struggling sailors, whose fine ship Poseidon has battered with wind and wave and smashed on the high seas. A few swim safely to the mainland out of the foaming surf, their bodies caked with brine; and blissfully they tread on solid land, saved from disaster. It was bliss like that for Penelope to see her husband once again. Her white arms round his neck never quite let go.

summer weekend with picnics, sandals, stripes, and brimmed hats. It is also a formidable force and can evoke a sense of terror.

Yet still it compels us, draws us, eliciting reverence and awe.

Maybe the two sides are of one piece, and the same hint of danger is contained in the delight. Perhaps the potential for terror is a part of the inexhaustible appeal. Or perhaps it has more to do with something deeper. "In fact," philosopher Peter Kreeft explains, "the sea is to the land what God is to everything—the surrounding ultimate mystery." We sense something, even if only in our subconscious, that pulls on the unbroken string connecting us to our ancient ancestors and stirs our universal and primordial desires and fears.

"If one does not know to which port one is sailing, no wind is favorable."

—SENECA THE YOUNGER

The sea draws us in but also makes us want to draw some of it into our homes. We want to live near it or at least bring its beauty inside—either a reflection of the tranquility and clarity or the drama and deep moodiness of the sea. It reminds us of adventure, recreation, or a quest for something beyond ourselves. Perhaps we simply want to remember a particular vacation or place and people we once knew. Even Odysseus planted an oar far from the sea among people who didn't recognize it. Farmers saw it as a winnowing fan, useful for separating wheat from chaff. Beyond its use or ornamentation, it was a stake in the ground, a sign that his trials were truly finished.

In many respects, the sea can feel like a man's world—most of the great literature on open waters is written by men about their adventures and quests, while women are left at home to "tend the hearths." But the bulk of this masculine experience doesn't need to leave women out of the conversation about the mystery and depths of the ocean, or of its beauty, bounty, and joy. Curiously, the sea can inform us more about who we are as women and how, in many ways, it reflects and mirrors deep elements about us that have slowly been eroded in our imaginations by today's culture.

"If you want to build a ship, don't drum up people to collect wood and don't assign them tasks and work, but rather teach them to long for the endless immensity of the sea."

–ANTOINE DE SAINT-EXUPERY

We live in a time of great confusion as human nature continues to be destabilized. The very thought of trying to define concepts like man, woman, and family have grown cloudy. This obscurity has serious consequences. We cannot become what we do not know. Humans have long needed northern stars—guides, midwives, saints, tutors, rabbis—to help

Katie Frye

O sea, I greet thee with a hard kombucha and a summer's paperback. Or perhaps a cold brew and a clutch of recipes for plotting out my week. But mostly I greet thee with a passel of children, some mine and some borrowed, their pinioned bodies sprung from the ebb and flow of the quotidian.

I watch them from my littoral perch, framing them between freshly varnished toes. They charge and hustle the waves, chase the sea spray, dive into the foamy barrels, harness boogie boards two apiece. Summer afternoons past encroach, reminding me of sand-tainted bottles and my husband hauling the stroller across the dunes and the baby's briny haunches daubed with tar. How much easier it all is now, how decadent, what frivolity with just a bottle of spray SPF and a week's worth of menu planning to contemplate; how indebted I am for this roiling reminder of my own mortality, this forced hiatus.

I tell my children, *If you swim far enough, you'll catch the Gulf and meet your grandmother as a little girl, hustling the sea crabs, chasing the piping plovers, diving into the currents.* I tell them she never needed a wetsuit.

I could tell them so much more about the sea: how it also ferried Odysseus and beguiled the Romantics and thwarted Ahab and will survive all this still until God wills it otherwise. Arnold had it all wrong: it *is* the Sea of Faith, lulling me into joy, drowning out all landlocked urgency, carrying me out into the wine dark with my children's ebullient shrieks.

CHAPTER 1

The She of the Sea

While writing this book, we were struck by how much the sea and life at sea separates men from women. Ships and boats have been manned by men, whether staying close to home in a bay or just offshore or those traveling the world in search of the yet unknown. What a different world it must have been from ours to watch a ship sail lower over the horizon, knowing your husband, son, or father was on it, wondering when or if you might see him again. There was no way to text or call or even send a letter. Wait and pray was about all a woman could do before her loved one(s) returned from war, from work, or from exploration. Although this is much changed today, the vast array of seafaring literature, journaling, and songs testify to the long, lonely ache of the unknown reunions of men and women. Perhaps it is some of this loneliness that led to the mythical creatures of nymphs and mermaids.

While a younger Hemingway often wrote of war and cities, with age, he turned to a story set at sea of an old man and a late, last battle.

"[Santiago] always thought of the sea as 'la mar' which is what people call her in Spanish when they love her. Sometimes those who love her say bad things of her but they are always said as though she were a woman." Hemingway continues, "Some of the younger fishermen, those who used buoys as floats for their lines and had motorboats, bought when the shark livers had brought much money, spoke of her as 'el mar' which is masculine. They spoke of her as a contestant or a place or even an enemy. But the old man always thought of her as feminine and as something that gave or withheld great favours, and if she did wild or wicked things it was because she could not help them. The moon affects her as it does a woman, he thought."

———————

"A woman knows the face of the man she loves
as a sailor knows the open sea."

–HONORE DE BALZAC

———————

While not universally so, the sea is generally thought of in feminine terms. Humanity has always desired to know the source and the routes by which all things came to be. The oldest myths have a common thread of a primordial water and a primordial mother that brought the earliest humans to life. Our earliest ancestors, bereft of most of our comforts, must have known keenly that nothing can live without water and that without women, there is no life. Both are present at any birth. This mythological thread is

Healing Springs

"It was the nearest thing to heaven," wailed Terry McKay to a speechless Nickie Ferrante. "You were there!"

So goes the teary climax of the 1957 film *An Affair to Remember*, featuring Deborah Kerr and Cary Grant.

The couple had met and unexpectedly fallen in love while crossing the Atlantic Ocean. As the ship moored, they made a pact to dissolve their other relationships and meet in six months at the top of the Empire State Building to dissolve their other relationships and for Ferrante to find a job.

Six months later to the day, Miss McKay, while looking up to the "nearest thing to heaven," is hit by a car, misses the rendezvous, and is left paralyzed and unable to meet Ferrante. He waits and waits but is devastated when she never shows up.

It is a common theme for the human heart to seek God and to reach for heaven at the highest heights, like Moses on the mountaintop. Our life is full of stories, pilgrimages, and prayers that manifest our desperate ascent to God.

But we don't always have to climb to find him. Often, what we really want is not to put ourselves higher but to "pull heaven down," to bring the goodness of God back down into the world.

There is, of course, no greater "pulling down heaven" than at the Mass, where the Lord joins us at a table through the hands of the priest before meeting us in our bodies in intimate communion.

But there is another common theme in Scripture that points to the grace of God dwelling in our midst: miraculous springs and healing waters. This significant symbol isn't found up high but quite literally down at our feet. We know the story of St. Bernadette at Lourdes, when our Lady asked her to dig in the dirt. The dirty mix of water and earth that gurgled

up quickly ran clear. This perpetual spring flows without end, and pilgrims continue to flock there to find healing, refreshment, faith, and peace. What started as a trickle prompted through St. Bernadette's humble faith and obedience led to an ocean of grace.

There are numerous lesser-known miraculous springs, most often associated with apparitions of the Blessed Mother, dating back all the way to the first century. These springs can be found all over the world: in India, Constantinople, Austria, Hungary, Italy, Spain, France, Portugal, the Philippines, Bolivia, and more.

One story from sixth-century Constantinople tells of two blind people who were led by a lady—later thought to be the Virgin Mary—to a spring, where they washed their eyes and were subsequently given sight. The spring continued to offer its healing waters and inspired the icon entitled "Life-Giving Spring of the Most Holy Theotokos."

A Byzantine Hymn honors the spring of salvation with this verse:

> O most favored by God, you confer on me the healing of your grace
> from your inexhaustible Spring. Therefore, since you gave birth incom-
> prehensibly to the Word, I implore you to refresh me with the dew of
> your grace that I might cry to you: Hail, O Water of salvation.

Dante also immortalized Mary as the living spring in the *Paradiso* book of *The Divine Comedy*:

> O Virgin Mother, daughter of your son, . . . Within your womb rekin-
> dled was the love that gave the warmth that did allow this flower to
> come to bloom within this timeless peace. For all up here you are the
> noonday torch of charity, and down on earth, for men, the living spring
> of their eternal hope. Not only does your loving kindness rush to those
> who ask for it, but often times it flows spontaneously before the plea.

strong in our own creation story, in Genesis and the story of Adam and of Eve, the mother of all.

Greek mythology has endured for centuries in part because there are wonders and mysteries in the world around us that even scientific advancements cannot fully encompass. We might know more today about the machinations and material contained in the sea, but still, we sense that there is more than matter and gravity and motion. There is mystery.

In Greek mythology, the sea nymphs—nereids—were the fifty daughters of Nereus and Doris. They were said to be young, beautiful, free spirited, and generally benevolent, protectors of castaways and entertainers of sailors. They are often depicted riding dolphins, reflecting their playful nature, but they could also be portrayed as threatening and vengeful.

"Carl Sandburg says that 'the sea hugs and will not let go.' Yes, but what are her arms? Notice the grammar: she is the subject and we are the object, rather than vice versa. How can the sea be active and the human spirit passive under her spell? We act on the sea with our ships, but she acts on our soul with her beauty."

—PETER KREEFT

Sirens, made famous in *The Odyssey*, were believed to be malevolent femme fatales who would lure sailors with their beautiful voices, putting them in a trance before leading them to their demise, either by dragging them into the depths of the sea or causing them to crash into rocks. Their mythos speaks to the inherent power women can exert over men and the potential threat implicit in their beauty as objects of desire.

Thetis, a goddess of the sea—whose son, Achilles, was prophesied to be bound for greatness—is characterized by her motherly love and guidance. As a goddess, and he a mortal, she has the sadness of knowing his tragic fate

before he does, and the inability to divert it despite her attempts to shield him. In one attempt, she dips Achilles in the river Styx to give him immortality, but her effort is thwarted by her grasp on his heel, thus leaving him with the vulnerability that would lead to his demise.

Story after story is replete with similar themes of a great mother's involvement in bringing about creature, nature, and life. Even the use of the phrase *Mother Nature* expresses this common way to describe the weather and the natural order. The idea of the great mother also points to the intense bond between child and mother, one that evokes the deepest of pains when it is absent, severed, neglected, or simply comes to an end with death.

Along with these early symbols of creation and procreation are the beautiful tasks assigned to woman—to hold, contain, feed, transform, and transport (even the word *transport* refers to the movement of ships from port to port). Women hold others in their arms, hearts, minds, and prayers. Consider the millions upon millions of men who've sailed out to sea and back, each carried in the minds and hearts of the women who loved them from the shore. But beyond that, still even today, like the sea, women help feed, and transform, and move—emotionally, intellectually, physically, and spiritually—those whom they meet, and particularly those for whom they care.

The sea, when she is in good temper or ill, can do all of these things: move, feed, transform, and transport those at her mercy. A sailor who engages her will not return the same person as when the voyage began. Mettle is tested and he is made wiser when faced with the choice to fight her or to get to know her ways and work with her. At times, the sea is a shrew he will never be able to tame. At others, she is a tender, healing, gentle mother.

But along with the sea itself, there is also the *she* of the ship. Boats, large and small, are usually assigned a female name. The steady ship offers a safe haven, a seal and protector between man and whatever nature and the deep blue sea have on offer: the immeasurable depths, the teeth of sharks, a surfacing whale, the surf's fury and the rain's pounding, the flash of lightning, the lashing of the wind, and the absence of freshwater.

Scripture speaks of this strong metaphor between a woman and a ship. "Like a merchant fleet, / she secures her provisions from afar" (Prv 31:14, NABRE). St. Albert the Great (1200–1281) wrote extensively on this single line of Scripture and spoke of the importance of a woman's character and virtue in his work *The Valiant Woman*. The merchant ship was likely a more powerful image for those who lived without weather prediction, GPS, and our advanced technology. Storms, lost ships, and faulty engineers were far more commonplace than in our day.

Speaking of the valiant woman, St. Albert suggests that "everything is found literally in a great ship that is said of her morally." His detailed comparison includes the prow and the stern, the belly and the keel, decks, mast, ropes and sails, and the anchor. He references the instructions for Noah's great ark, "Thou shalt pitch it within and without" (Gen. 6:14 DRA). She, Albert explains, "is preserved with the pitch of charity, on the inside by the love of God and on the outside by love of neighbor."

St. Albert goes on to explain in a very detailed fashion other character elements of a woman. Far beyond a mere reduction of the valiant woman as someone servile or merely a cauldron of emotions or fancy, Albert makes quite plain the depths and gifts that women have at their disposal:

The Moody Sea

I grew up an hour away from the Oregon coast, with its long sandy beaches and great stretches of dunes. It was more common than not to encounter days when thick fog rolled in, or when it was raining sideways with fierce wind. Sometimes, the fog was so thick one could scarcely tell there was a vast ocean behind it if not for the sound of the tides splashing the shore.

I don't think there was ever a day I wore just a bathing suit on the beach; it was always too cold between the wind and the surf. But the real battle was with the wind and the sand. The sand got everywhere—in your hair, down your back, across your neck. Shelters were dug and maybe a small fire enkindled to protect us from the wind's chilly lashing.

On soft days, the long sandy beaches felt like a friend who welcomed you into her living room and showed off her new treasures—with shell-pocked sand, driftwood curiosities, and other flotsam and jetsam that dotted the beach. There was kelp and other seaweeds, some over twenty feet long, that washed ashore, along with sand dollars, other shells, and jelly fish. Even spouting whales could be spotted as they migrated north and then south again. We relished those gentle days when she let us savor her bounty.

More often than not, the weather was angry and prickly. Finding beach reading didn't mean the book to read on the beach but the books to take along when it was just too cold and windy to head outdoors. When we did venture out, it felt like visiting a cantankerous aunt who resented your presence, requiring tight hoods and heavy jeans to keep warm. And, of course, bare feet—somehow, not putting your toes in the sand felt like you didn't really make it to the beach at all.

We knew her moods keenly and did what we could to overcome her temper. But it wasn't the worst thing to retreat when her rage was just too strong and watch her drama unfold before us from the comfort of a cozy living room with a fire and a good book.

The belly or the hold of the ship is the natural affections, namely, hope, despair, and joy. The lookout of the ship is the purgation of confession; the storeroom is the reminder through meditation; the cabin the secrets of conscience; the upper deck the confidence of security; the broad deck for walking is the passing of contemplation; the foremast is the height of faith; the rear mast is understanding, since in divine matters understanding follows faith. The ropes that spread the sail are wonder at the ultimate truths of faith which are known, as it were, through certain rings of metaphors and figures. The rudders signify authorities and revelation, since St. Augustine says, "What we believe ought to be based on authority." On the mast, which is understanding, are the ropes of reason by which the sails are connected to the mast through the rings and clasps of study and reading, and these sails are spread by the winds of disputation and teaching.

"Mother. That's what the sea was for all of us until a few millennia ago."

—PETER KREEFT

There are several remarkable things about this passage. The first is that it certainly doesn't paint a picture of the passive women often associated with medieval times. Rather, it is a woman who is educated, who knows she is loved, and who uses everything available to her to make good and wise decisions.

The second remarkable thing is how sharp a contrast it is to the present limited view we have of womanhood. Today, we are tossed around on the stormy seas of our emotions or the emotions of others without the anchor

Mary McClusky

After her seventh child turned two, my mother needed a well-deserved break. She drove from Jackson, Michigan "to find a sandy piece of beach" and landed at a log cabin on the shore of Lake Superior. After a week by herself reading, praying, and renewing her love of sketching, she brought my dad and all the kids up every summer of our childhoods.

I have fond memories of combing the rocky beach for agates, roasting marshmallows over a fire at sunset, and driving to the Jampot to buy baked goodies from the Byzantine monks who chose this remote part of Michigan to live, work, and pray.

To get her annual sabbatical, Mom eventually had to spend her week in the Upper Peninsula during the winter—even chopping a hole in frozen Lake Superior to retrieve water.

I received my sense of adventure and love of travel from my mother. Most importantly, she taught me there's nothing like the power of nature and some time alone reflecting by the water to restore the soul and to reconnect with God and his many gifts.

of faith, objective truth, or even reason. These things have been scuttled for the ratings-grabbing pop culture featuring lust, anger, tears, fear, and outrage, all of which serve the anemic ideals of radical autonomy and human desire: "I want it, therefore, it must be so." The effect is to lock us up, like a child, in all want and no restraint.

Peter's Barque

The ship metaphor carries over into church architecture and even the Church itself. In a twelfth-century homily, the Scottish monk and theologian Richard of St. Victor said, "The world, dear brethren, is a sea. Because like the sea it stinks, swells, is false and unstable. . . . It is, therefore, brethren necessary that we should have a ship, and all that belongs to it, if we wish to cross the perilous sea without danger."

In church architecture, the central and largest part of the church is called the nave, which refers to the Latin for ship, from which we also get the word *navy*. Mother Church, also a she, embraces those on their way—much like the embrace of the arms of St. Peter's Square—often sailing through the stormy seas of life, protecting them, feeding them, and bringing them home.

The Church is sometimes depicted with Christ or St. Peter as the helmsman surrounded by the faithful. The metaphor dots Scripture, history, and art from the ark of Noah to the barque of Peter to the boat of Jude. Although it is not known which thirteenth-century pope said it—either Gregory IX or Innocent IV—one of them captured the notion well: "In vain you strive to submerge the ship of Peter—this vessel rocks but is never submerged."

Maria Gerwel

Translated from Polish by Wojciech Gerwel

The attic in my family's home was tall with a pyramid-shaped roof, accessible by ladder. Climbing up to it with heavy large binoculars was quite a feat for a young child, but it was the only place to view the sea. Whenever my beloved father, a captain in merchant marine, was returning from a voyage, my mum used to order me to watch the Gdanńsk roadstead and notify her the moment his ship was being led into the harbor. Then my mother would take all three of us to greet him. Those were wonderful moments. His presence at home was a great feast for our family. Sadly, he died suddenly when I was twenty-two, much too soon.

My father, my uncle, and my cousins were merchant marine captains. In childhood, during family celebrations, they would gather around the table and share recollections about sailing in convoys during World War II.

As a young woman, I went to work at sea. After I got my diploma, I married a young officer. We sailed together for several years. Sunrises, sunsets, stormy seas, and calm waters—it all has irresistible appeal and renders one's heart more sensitive to beauty. Waking up each day in a different place on earth, looking at world events in perspective, delving into silence—such things greatly kindle the soul's upward yearning.

Then the children were born and again, as I had once awaited my father, I now waited at home for my husband to return.

When we lived behind the Iron Curtain, the sea was a window to the world. As seamen, we were able to visit many beautiful places and earn a salary significantly above the national average. This labor gave us satisfaction, even if it was extraordinarily difficult. Someone once said that people could be divided into three categories: the living, the dead, and the ones at sea.

I live two hundred yards from the sea. For thirty-three years, I have been walking along its shore every day at dawn and in the evening. During his holidays at home, my husband was eager to accompany me on these walks. Later, when he retired, we walked together hand in hand for a year until his death. For both of us, the sea was a great love.

For several years now, my husband has been gone. Also gone are the people of the sea who had surrounded me in my life. As a child, I would fall asleep on the floor at the great helm on the captain's bridge, and afterwards, Dad would carry me to the cabin. More and more often, I think back to memories like these and all the beautiful moments in my life, and most of them have the scent of the sea.

CHAPTER 2

Reverence and Obedience

Having spent her formative years near the ocean, my dear friend and her family of twelve relocated to a landlocked state. When she returns for a rare visit, there is a palpable joy that accompanies her reunion with the ocean. She breathes in the salty air and, now with a family of her own, carves out time to share her love of the sea with her husband and children.

On a recent visit, I asked her what it was about the sea that meant so much to her.

"Powerful obedience," she responded without hesitation.

The ocean is vast and unruly, yet still there is a marvelous sort of powerful obedience in the way the waves roll in and recede out, heeding the laws that govern it day after day.

We often think of *our* need to respect the ocean, sometimes forgetting that the sea is respecting something higher as well. Our reverence for the great things of nature is not meant to stop there. The sea is not a god; she is also bound by things outside of herself, despite her immensity and wildness. The vast power of the sea is subordinate to gravity, the moon, the wind, the shifting tectonic forces of the earth, and the laws of nature and nature's God. And the sea is more glorious because of her obedience.

"Sailors, with their built in sense of order, service and discipline, should really be running the world."

–NICHOLAS MONSARRAT

Even in the smaller, more hidden parts of nature, we can see this sort of simple harmony of obedience to purpose. In her charming essay "Living Like Weasels," Annie Dillard writes of an encounter with one such small creature on a walk and how it prompted her to consider the goodness of living as we are meant. She realized that our free choices are most maximized in conformity with our mission. A weasel, she thought, exemplified this sort of simplicity through its purpose-driven actions. We, on the other hand, complicate things by lionizing *the sheer ability to make choices* rather than choosing something in accord with our purpose.

"People take vows of poverty, chastity, and obedience—even of silence—by choice. The thing is to stalk your calling in a certain skilled and supple way. . . . A weasel doesn't 'attack' anything; a weasel lives as he's meant to, yielding at every moment to the perfect freedom of single necessity." Rather

Waterfall

When I was expecting my fourth child, after having suffered a number of traumatic losses already, another young mother commiserated with me that pregnancy felt a bit like approaching a waterfall. The machinations of my body were stretching and articulating as they prepared for the impending, dramatic rush of childbirth in all its glorious beauty and terrifying surrender. In cartoon renderings, being swept away into a waterfall is entirely survivable, albeit scary. The reality of going over a waterfall, of course, would be harrowing, with boulders and shock and likely death. But in our imaginations, it's easy to imagine it being a softer experience where we do not freefall but rather are carried along and down, with the cushion of a pool waiting to receive us.

I think the mother meant the analogy in the gentler way, and it seems an apt one. The perspective from the top of a waterfall is terrifying—the height, the rush of water, the total lack of control, the impending escalation of pain, the pushing force of nature, the crashing gravity of it all. But to encounter a waterfall from below feels something like finding a mystical pocket of the world—a unicorn in the forest. From below, we can see the rush of water as delightful, musical. Perhaps part of our delight at the bottom is knowing that of the two perspectives, ours is the better one to have. To see the beauty and not feel the fear.

Our first pregnancy came quickly after we married. We were young, and poor, and scared. All of that disappeared when our daughter came. After the strained and messy noise of childbirth, there is a marvelous silence. The staff leaves, the lights are dimmed. Three people lay looking and dopily grinning at one another, or at least two are—the little grins come later. What exactly about this glorious, tiny, ballerina baby were we afraid of?

As kids get older and birth gets further away, we sit in that perspective, at the bottom of the fall, near the pool, surrounded by mystery. What a wonder to have traveled down that waterfall, gripping our sides and one another, banged and bruised, only to find ourselves on this verdant planet below.

than fighting against our nature, we can, like the weasel, freely choose to devote ourselves to it. Dillard goes on, "I think it would be well, and proper, and obedient, and pure, to grasp your one necessity and not let it go, to dangle from it limp wherever it takes you."

"Roll on, deep and dark blue ocean, roll.
Ten thousand fleets sweep over thee in vain.
Man marks the earth with ruin,
but his control stops with the shore."

–LORD BYRON

I like the word *grasp* in this context; it speaks to both our intellect and our will. We must understand our purpose and commit to it. Most lovers of the sea will say that there is no reverence without knowledge—knowledge of the nature of the sea and respect for our inability to control it. Surfers speak of the way a wave can consume you, spit you out, and slam you against a jagged reef. A smart surfer, or sailor or ship captain, knows that the ocean has patterns and cycles. There are elements to consider and seasons to anticipate. He must have a reverence for all of these because of our smallness in comparison to its grandness.

One of the first things children learn when encountering the ocean is that it is much bigger than they are. As a child, when first confronted by a wave higher than my head, I panicked and got slapped off my feet. Water

flooded my nose and my face turned red and raw. I quickly learned that there are two better options: jump and ride the surface of the wave or dive under the turmoil of it to find the stillness below. There is a sort of respect it demands, and our respect of it leads to greater harmony with it.

———————

"I often thought my constitution would never endure the work I had to do, (but) the Lord said to me: 'Daughter, obedience gives strength.'"

–ST. TERESA OF AVILA

———————

There is a tremendous strength in reverence and obedience. Obedience leads to deeper reverence, and reverence back to a deeper understanding of obedience. The two together protect us from peril, hubris, and ingratitude.

It is no surprise, then, that as we realize the good of living in harmony with respect to nature in one way, so we might also come to see the good of living in harmony with nature in other aspects of life. Somehow, we tend to forget that our bodies are a part of our very nature, with clues into how we might live and hints at the contours and content of our humanity and happiness. There is a givenness to them that we deny at our own peril.

The way in which we do or do not live in harmony with our human nature bleeds into other aspects of natural life. This suggests that we ought not compartmentalize these things. As in the past, the majority of marine pollution arises from land-based sources. The difference today is that plastics, pesticides, pharmaceuticals, waste, runoff, and sewage all contribute to a wide array of pollutants that don't decompose in the same way as organic matter. Some are more harmful to the biology of the sea than others, but all are unwelcome, and some may surprise us. An active ingredient in the birth control pill, for example, travels

Kimberly Cook

The promise of the wild island country of New Zealand, with its black sand beaches, geothermal pools, volcanic mountains, and sea caves, had long pulled at my heart. Years ago, when a friend asked where we would go if we could anywhere in the world, my future husband and I both named it immediately and in unison. I still remember the way we looked at each other after we blurted out our answer. It was unusual to find another person who was as deeply drawn by the untamed wilderness of New Zealand's rugged mountain peaks rising out of fields of saturated wildflowers. We were soulmates who longed to kayak the glassy fjords decorated with penguins and seals.

Our dream became a reality on our honeymoon, introducing us into the great journey of marriage. As we drove across the two islands of New Zealand in a camper van with nothing but the necessities and hearts full of adventure, we learned the value of living with simplicity and beauty. Together, we hiked challenging slopes and icy blue glaciers, often eating camp-stove meals on beaches as the sun set. We learned to rely on God, each other, and the kindness of strangers. These lessons, absorbed in such a dramatic setting, have become a theme threaded throughout our marriage, even amid the mundane tasks that come with married life. We learned to look for the joy in simplicity, the value of friendship, a sense of adventure, and the awe of God.

Moby Dick: "A gentle joyousness—a mighty mildness of repose in swift-ness, invested the gliding whale."

For me, to rest in the rise and fall of an infinitesimal swell of the Pacific is to dwell, if only for a time, in the waters over which the spirit hovered in the very beginning, to have a glimpse into the firmament of the waters, to be thereby with God in the world before he made Adam, muzzle to muzzle with his beloved creatures of the deep, "the great sea monsters and every living thing that moves, with which the waters swam, according to their kinds," unconquerable and immense. It means to be loved by a love that is beyond human or terrestrial—dangerous, unpredictable, entirely at home. Honored and alive.

CHAPTER 3

Mystery and Depth

Several years ago, my husband and I had the opportunity to take a company-sponsored trip to Cancún. While the resort was beautiful, it lacked some of the cultural and natural authenticity we wanted to discover and explore. Thankfully, an eight-mile ferry trip to Isla Mujeres provided an opportunity for adventure.

At only five miles long and four hundred yards at its widest point, the narrow island gives one the feeling of being at the sea everywhere you go. Despite the watery border, people seem unencumbered by boundaries. Noticeably absent are lane markers in the streets, either drawn or acknowledged. Architectural elements are painted boldly and bravely, my favorite being the reoccurring deep, bougainvillea pink walls. Even the island's star adventure attraction—deep sea diving—bespeaks of a certain comfortability with penetrating below the surface and an intuitive acknowledgment of the reality of what lies beyond.

The name *Isla Mujeres* translates to "Island of Women." It is derived from Spanish settlers who discovered idols to Mayan goddesses there, as well as from the prevalence of female inhabitants while the men were out at sea. In 1890, fishermen discovered wood and porcelain statues of the Blessed Mother on the tip of Quintana Roo. One of the fishermen took a statue to his home on the island, where our Lady was enshrined in a small chapel made of palms. Years later, the decision was made to move her to a church, but the statue had inexplicably become far heavier and more challenging to move. When she was finally relocated, the palm shrine burst into flames, to the obvious astonishment of onlookers. She's now in residence at the Catholic church of the Immaculate Conception, and local legend claims numerous sightings of her walking along the sea at dawn.

―――――――

"'Deep calls unto deep.' The sea without
calls to our sea within, and the tides of our spirit
are pulled by the gravity of the sea."

—PETER KREEFT

―――――――

In the modern secular world, with our tidy grids and air conditioning, it is easy to get used to feeling skeptical of the reality of the immaterial. On Isla Mujeres, the elements and the sea feel more present than the land. Like the watery border, religion and mystery surround you there. Inhabitants, secular

and not, reference Holy Week as we would reference spring, and everyone comes out for the eleven-day festival in December celebrating the feast of the Immaculate Conception, the island's patroness.

There's a chance that a culture so steeped in religion can become ritualistic or merely superstitious, a veneer of the old faith masking a hollow core. Obviously, I couldn't discern where the island dwellers fell on such a spectrum in one day. I'm sure, like anywhere, it's a mix. Perhaps their life, so surrounded by the wildness of nature, has caused the mysteries of religion and an awareness of mortality to be embedded deeply within them.

No matter where we live, we can cultivate that same sort of wonder and awareness. Besides engaging us intellectually and corporeally, our faith prompts us to foster a deep sense of supernatural wonder, a sense we should feel in our bones. It is in encountering that wonder, that mystery, that we feel most fully human. In engaging in the things below the surface—both the horror and the delight, the mystery and the depth—we become more deeply alive.

"I find the great thing in this world is not so much
where we stand, as in what direction we are moving:
To reach the port of heaven, we must sail sometimes
with the wind and sometimes against it, but
we must sail, and not drift, nor lie at anchor."

—OLIVER WENDELL HOLMES, JR.

One of Jesus's tasks on earth was to "make all things new" (Rv 21:5). Creation needed to be restored to what it was meant to be, like Eden, and not left caked over with a jumble of pagan ritual and meaning. G. K. Chesterton speaks of the gargantuan task to rid every bit of creation of its pagan bonds. The thorough scouring, he postulates, happened with the fall of Rome and the

Jane and the Sea

Jane Austen's life and writing were punctuated by the sea. In *Emma*, the title character is loveable but blind to her own faults and oblivious to her blindness. Though privileged, Emma has never had the chance to see the sea. It is not until the end approaches, having been chastened and deepened and in the happiness of finding real love, that she is given her first glimpse of the coast. In this way, Austen seems to use the sea as a sort of necessary piece of human life, a piece whose omission in our vision cries out for resolution.

Seaside resorts, established and made fashionable in eighteenth-century England, play varying backdrops in her novels. The sea can serve to highlight a perilous period in life, such as Georgiana Darcy's ill-fated elopement with Mr. Wickham at Ramsgate. In *Pride and Prejudice*, the seaside town of Brighton is considered irresistibly delightful, but one of mere frivolity. Elizabeth Bennett frets that her young and intemperate sister Lydia will abandon any lingering restraint on her conduct should she spend a summer at Brighton. In her own life, Austen often longed to be near the sea, a longing that was satisfied at various times.

Breathing in sea air served as a tonic of sorts. The sea in her day was understood to have healing properties. It also held a more obvious appeal. For the Austen family in 1801, landlocked in the heat (and stench) of a summer in Bath, the prospect of accepting an offer to make their summer home by the sea in Sidmouth was too appealing to resist. When a competing invitation from their clergyman, cousin Edward Cooper, came beckoning them to his lovely, but not seaside, abode for the summer, Austen replied that he was "so kind as to want us all to come to Hamstall this summer, instead of going to the sea, but we are not so kind as to mean to do it." Austen went on, "The summer after, if you please, Mr. Cooper, but for the present we greatly prefer the sea to all our relations." It is a line easily imagined coming from the slightly smirking mouth of Miss Elizabeth Bennett, perhaps addressed to her sniveling cousin Mr. Collins.

Elizabeth, a lover of nature, but eminently too reasonable to not see the dangers within, would have had just the sort of clear-eyed perspective on the sea as did her author. Austen seemed to understand the sea and human dynamics somewhat similarly, both being mercurial and beguiling. In her stories, nature often serves to highlight or underscore human nature. There is the surface layer full of lighthearted banter and playful wit dancing off one another. But no one would accuse Austen of remaining on the surface. Rather, the visible layer of each character reveals—or eventually unmasks—what lurks beneath. Though she seems to delight in playfulness, a life lived merely in frivolity is exposed in her novels as condemnable. But to never behold the sea is a limitation not befitting of a life in full either.

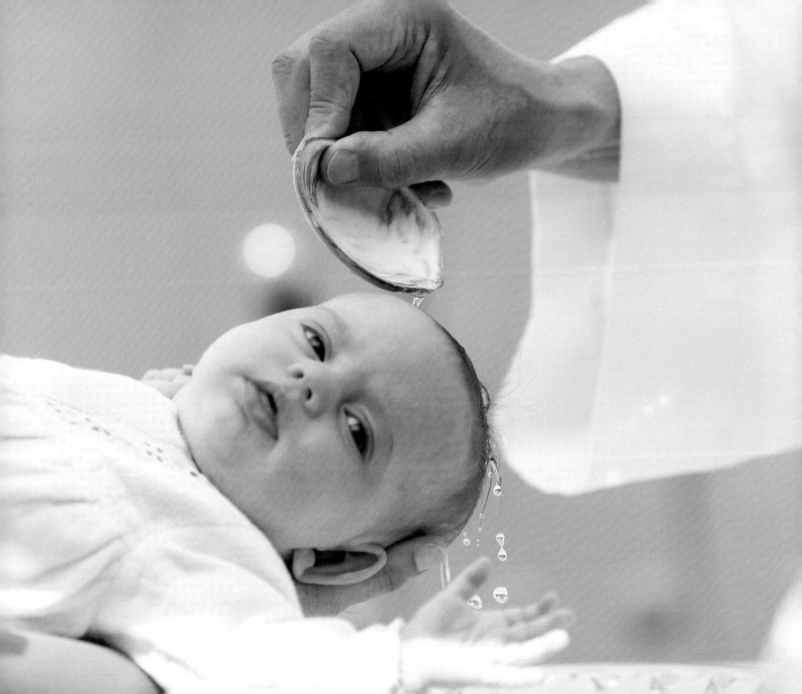

ensuing dark ages that left creation free to be seen in a Christian light rather than through pagan darkness. The first element to be purified was water, transformed through Christ's baptism in the Jordan by John the Baptist. Through this, water was redeemed and made new for all the world to be baptized.

"The sea drives truth into a man like salt."

—HILAIRE BELLOC

That scouring of water and that baptism on the banks of the Jordan opened fresh to every man and woman the right relationship to God, which had been squandered and separated by our first parents. While the pagans had deep and complicated rituals that involved animal sacrifice and the offerings of food, wine, and goods, our ritual or recipe for return couldn't be simpler: water and a prayer. Paired with the sacred words of the sacramental rite, one drop of water gives a soul the capacity to enter into the ocean of God's grace and to discover the depths of eternal life in ways completely unknown in the ancient world.

The relationship between Jesus and water didn't stop at the Jordan's banks. As Tertullian pointed out in the third century, water is vital to Christ's salvific work:

> Wherever Christ is, there is water: He Himself is baptized in
> water; when called to a marriage He inaugurates with water

the first rudiments of His power; when engaged in conversation He invites those who are athirst to come to His everlasting water; when teaching of charity He approves of a cup of water offered to a little one as one of the works of affection; He walks upon the water; by His own choice He crosses over the water; with water He makes Himself a servant to His disciples. He continues His witness to the Baptism right on to His Passion; when He is given up to the Cross, water is in evidence, as Pilate's hands are aware; when He receives a wound water burst forth from His side, as the soldier's spear can tell.

Jesus communicates to us that water isn't a trifle but rather a deeply meaningful way to communicate God's grace, healing, and love.

Buried Treasure

There are few things that can hold our attention like a deep-sea treasure or the message in a bottle that washes ashore decades after it was tossed into the ocean. Millions of dollars are spent searching for long lost ships, some just below the surface and others miles deep. Found in various stages of decay, any bounty recovered is a thing of fascination, raising all sorts of questions: How did the ship sink? When did it sink? What was on the ship? Who went down with it? Images come to mind of perhaps the last hands to have handled what is recovered—maybe amphora filled with oil or wine, chests with golden coins, or even the more mundane wares of everyday life, like spoons and broken cups. We are often left with more questions than answers, but the imagination can go wild filling in the blanks, wishing that the submerged timbers, the barnacled bows, or chipped teacups could just tell us even part of their story.

"Just as there are things about a woman
that only a woman can understand,
there are things about the sea that
only the sea within me can understand."

–PETER KREEFT

We are used to thinking of women as being mysterious. Men often comment on how they will never understand them. And while it may be a cliche, there is some truth to the idea that men seem to be far less complex than women. At any given moment, a wife might be thinking about her to-dos, worrying about her children, wondering if she hurt her friend's feelings, and curious what her husband might be thinking. Men's minds don't often operate in these circuitous ways. When prompted to share his thoughts, it might be in regard to dinner, or the game, or work. Truly, one is not better or worse; they are just different tendencies that can be directed for good or for bad.

But women are mysterious not only because our brains are hardwired differently than men's. There is something deeper and more interesting at work that we often miss because of the constant radio static buzzing in our culture over the battle of sexes.

God whispers in the attentive soul. Perhaps a woman is plain or unassuming on the outside, but buried deep within are hidden treasures she guards cautiously, never to be thrown before swine. Part of a man's duty is to protect these unplumbed depths, while part of her duty is to discover them.

"If the highest aim of a captain
were to preserve his ship,
he would keep it in port forever."

–THOMAS AQUINAS

It is no accident that the first to know of Jesus's great works were women: Mary at the Incarnation and the wedding feast of Cana, the Marys at the foot of the cross, and Mary Magdalene at the tomb. Women, like the deep waters of the ocean, can receive treasure. We store it, hold it, ponder it, preserve it, transport it, and then, when it is time, surrender or offer it for someone's benefit.

Every culture has had its share of shallow women, as well as a much smaller share of deep women. The difference isn't simply one of temperament but seems to sit squarely upon the relationship a woman has with God. The superficiality of many women—the gossips, those that flit about looking for a new diversion or the latest trends—isn't really who they are made to be.

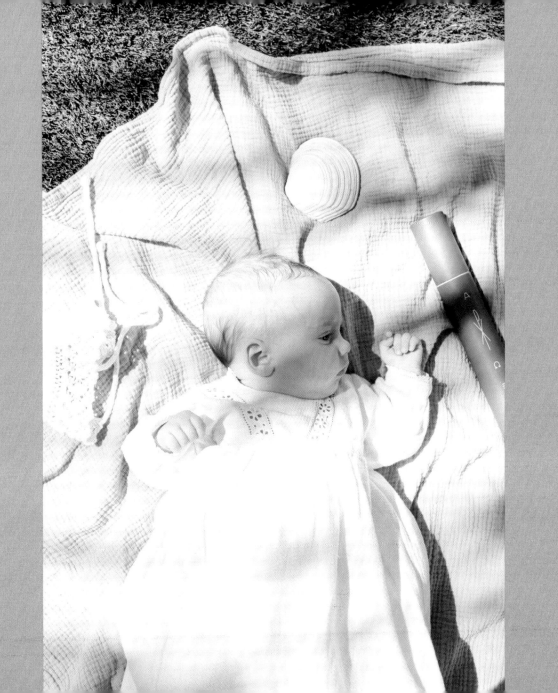

The sand and dark water and sediment of sin must be cleared away in order that they might go deeper to discover truth and treasure.

Christ reveals this age-old pattern when he meets the woman at the well:

> There came a woman of Samar'ia to draw water. Jesus said to her, "Give me a drink." For his disciples had gone away into the city to buy food. The Samaritan woman said to him, "How is it that you, a Jew, ask a drink of me, a woman of Samar'ia?" For Jews have no dealings with Samaritans. Jesus answered her, "If you knew the gift of God, and who it is that is saying to you, 'Give me a drink,' you would have asked him, and he would have given you living water." The woman said to him, "Sir, you have nothing to draw with, and the well is deep; where do you get that living water? Are you greater than our father Jacob, who gave us the well, and drank from it himself, and his sons, and his cattle?" Jesus said to her, "Every one who drinks of this water will thirst again, but whoever drinks of the water that I shall give him will never thirst; the water that I shall give him will become in him a spring of water welling up to eternal life." (Jn 4:7–14)

He knows she is coming to the well at midday because she is ashamed and wants to avoid the other women who gather at the well earlier before the day is too hot. Jesus wants her to go deeper, to give her more than she even knows how to ask for. He wants to help her find something much more precious than all the anxiety, grief, regret, resentment, and pain she carries

Laura Camacho

The beaches up and down the South Carolina lowcountry are not ideal postcard material. The water is not clear or turquoise, the sand is not white, and there are no glamorous palm trees or impressive rock formations. The murky green water doesn't let me see the mysterious things (creatures, seaweed, sharks?) that brush against my feet and legs. The sand, well, it's sand colored. The beaches sport seashells, but they're small and usually broken. There is no shade to save me from the beating sun.

And yet it soothes my fraying nerves.

I can be at my favorite beach in fifteen minutes. Driving over the bridge to Sullivan's Island, I see the marsh, the boats, the harbor, maybe a setting sun, and the statue of the Virgin that tops Stella Maris Catholic Church, our Lady's eyes watching Charleston Harbor. I breathe in deeply, exhale slowly, and once more give thanks that I live here.

Lowering the windows, I get a whiff of pluff mud, the secret ingredient of lowcountry beaches. Pluff mud, a rich sediment in our saltwater marshes, proffers its ecosystem food and shelter. It is the byproduct of mixing algae, decaying organisms, and dead plants. Not what you think of as attractive ingredients.

And yet, these lowcountry beaches delight the eyes. The wind, the waves, and the winged creatures create ultimate calming sounds. The sand massages the soles of your feet. But the coup de grace, the signature experience, non-plus ultra of the low country shore is the pluff mud scent that rises from the marshes.

That is the smell that unwaveringly communicates all will be well.

inside. He is asking her to find *him*, to find the kind of water—of grace, love, and mercy—that will quench her true and most ardent thirst. The well water will quench her thirst for now. But the living water will quench her thirst for eternity. This is the pearl—the greatest treasure of the sea—that reveals the pitifulness of a life spent slogging through sediment.

This living water is prefigured in the Old Testament. Ezekiel speaks of a great river:

> And wherever the river goes every living creature which swarms will live, and there will be very many fish; for this water goes there, that the waters of the sea may become fresh; so everything will live where the river goes. Fishermen will stand beside the sea; from En-ge′di to En-eg′laim it will be a place for the spreading of nets; its fish will be of very many kinds, like the fish of the Great Sea. But its swamps and marshes will not become fresh; they are to be left for salt. And on the banks, on both sides of the river, there will grow all kinds of trees for food. Their leaves will not wither nor their fruit fail, but they will bear fresh fruit every month, because the water for them flows from the sanctuary. Their fruit will be for food, and their leaves for healing. (Ez 47: 9–12)

This is why we are asked to do the hard work of scrutinizing our behavior, confessing our sins, and trying to grow in virtue—not because it helps God but because it helps us. In this clearing, we see things we could never imagine when we were surrendered to the tide. With it comes the capacity to say with St. Catherine of Siena, "You [the Trinity] are like a deep sea; the more I enter you the more I discover, and the more I discover the more I seek you." God becomes both the thirst but also the living water that quenches the thirst.

It is easy to think that Christ's ocean of mercy isn't meant for us, especially as we grow comfortable in our messes and habits. But it is. "My daughter," Jesus said to St. Faustina, "tell the whole world about My inconceivable mercy. . . . I pour out a whole ocean of graces upon those souls who approach the fount of My mercy."

CHAPTER 4

Joy and Beauty

We live in a sleepy beach town. Every summer, one particular beach becomes a second home to many in our community, especially on Sunday afternoons as large groups of friends and families gather to master the art of making the beach a temporary home. If you drive your family of ten half an hour to get to the coast and then navigate parking and carting people and things down the numerous steps to the sand, you're going to want to make it worth your while. Coolers and chairs and children and toys are carried, and blankets are laid down staking your home base for the day. Pop-up tents with pack-and-plays are set up so that babies can take their afternoon naps, and grills are fired up on low folding tables as the dinner hour nears.

No one is ever bored. Toddlers, teens, and parents alike frolic, chat, read, swim, nap, and throw frisbees. At some point, someone remarks about what a godsend this is for all—to gather, be outside, be active, and just be

Food

What food we consume by the water can vary from sandwiches and chips, grilled burgers and hot dogs, to more refined bites of seafood and beverage pairings—oysters, ceviche, a crisp white wine.

Picnicking on sand requires some effort and precautionary measures—a low table can keep things from being doused with sand or trampled by small children. For those fortunate enough to have access to a home on the sea, or perhaps a favorite restaurant mere steps from the sand, meals can be a fancier affair.

What is considered the quintessential sea fare will change depending on the locale. New England lobster rolls and clams, West Coast fish tacos and breakfast burritos, Maryland blue crabs, Louisiana crawfish and Cajun crab, salmon and Dungeness crab from the Pacific Northwest, and shrimp and grits in the Carolinas all can be considered quintessential coastal cuisine. Oysters of any sort are found in any seaside locale worth its salt.

Taste, along with smell, is immediately evocative of a memory—able to transport us with one bite to a time and place from our past. We can see this in the negative when a formerly beloved food will become repugnant after having experienced food sickness from it (or after an inexplicable pregnancy aversion to it).

While there is a certain survival instinct at play in such scenarios, there is also the sweet rush of a delightful memory that can be triggered by a bite of food. The part of the brain called the hippocampus is closely associated with smell and emotion, both of which are closely connected to the experience of eating. We might be transported to childhood vacations with a bite of saltwater taffy, or to a favorite trip to San Francisco with the smell of fresh sourdough bread and chowder. The vibrancy with which we tend to experience food while in a memorable place forms an indelible memory that can be stored and revivified in an instant, even decades later.

together—all with no entrance fee required. The preparation and subsequent breakdown are done with the awareness that the gain far exceeded the effort.

————

"Her restless waves give rest to my soul.
She restores my soul.
She restores my past by washing it away."

–PETER KREEFT

————

Historically, great effort has been expended by families to recreate at the ocean. Following the summer migration patterns the world over, mothers and children would go to the shore first, setting up house for the summer months, with fathers to follow for the weekend. One train route in Oregon connecting Portland and the small town of Seaside, established before a highway was constructed, became known as "daddy trains" because the husbands would make their way to the beach for the weekend and then return Sunday afternoon to prepare for the workweek. Even though the transportation, fabrics, and fashions of the beach have changed radically, there is something ever nostalgic and new in the memory and hope of a warm day at the sea.

Youthfulness

The philosopher Peter Kreeft has long spoken and written of his abiding love for the sea. He sums up what the sea does to him with one word: *magic*. His exuberance as he describes how the sea affects him is reminiscent of the experience of being a child at play and the unrestraint that comes from being pulled completely outside ourselves.

Souvenirs

I recall as a child trying to pick out the perfect souvenir from the rows of beach kitsch—perhaps a bottle with a piece of paper with the beach name on it? Or saltwater taffy? A pencil? Coin purse? And on and on it went as the wadded-up dollar bills got warmer in my hand through the intense selection process. I don't think any of those carefully chosen trinkets made it to adulthood with me.

But I do have one souvenir that I hope my daughter will treasure when she is an adult. One Christmas, we made our way to a friend's beach home in Delaware. His wife had recently passed and he was trying to keep himself surrounded by friends. Any comfort we could give him was more than returned by his gracious hospitality. The kids especially enjoyed his home, which had a layout highly conducive to endless games of hide-and-go-seek.

As I was putting the baby to sleep, I overheard our friend talking to my then six-year-old daughter. "Why don't you pick one out?" I heard him say. I learned later that, at his bidding, she had chosen a beautifully formed conch shell rescued from a nearby beach to take home with us. It is now displayed in our home, and to this day, I always think of our dear friend, who passed away a year after our visit. It reminds me of his warmth, his graciousness, his generosity, and his friendship. And it reminds me to pray for him. It is the perfect souvenir.

"Watch the very young at the beach," he says. "They play in the Great Mother's untiring waves and become almost as heedless of time as She is. How remarkable that those who are bored the quickest with everything else—the young, the ones with the shortest attention spans—are always the last to want to leave the beach!"

"Come, let us give a little time to folly . . .
and even in a melancholy day let us
find time for an hour of pleasure."

–ST. BONAVENTURE

The sea's waves slap and throw and lift us in ways that pull us from our sense of control. Any lingering feeling of decorum is dashed as we are flipped and jostled, tumbling and turning in her power. It prompts us to set aside our self-consciousness, our cares, our distractions. The sea is totally immersive. We can be swept away by it either literally or figuratively. It absorbs our focus as well as our bodies, our sightline, our minds. There is some danger there, but there is also the possibility of great joy.

A person in love, no matter his age, is imbued with a sort of youthfulness that makes life seem more vibrant. Kreeft notes that the sea affects him similarly. "A good lover gives you more energy to love *everything*. A bad lover

drains away your energy into himself like a vampire. The sea is a good lover to me."

There is a sweetness and an abandonment in the blush of young love. We sacrifice eagerly without reservation. We want to withhold nothing and desire little more than the object of our love. We naturally aim to make our beloved happy, to commit our futures and presents, to reveal our pasts. The youthful character of love is not enough for a lifetime, but it is also not to be

Emily Malloy

Tiny grains of sand sift between my toes as my breathing steadies to take in the fragrant, salty breeze where land meets the sea. I cannot help but linger and permit my senses to run wild. The sea is both bold and untamed, yet its consumable bounty is so very delicate. Only seafood is capable of being both flaky and moist. These gifts of flaky freshness are seasoned by the same immensity that salts the air. I can almost taste the fish as I take it all in.

Slow living is essential, as seafood is an elegant cuisine that begs to be savored. The very nature by which seafood is caught forces the fisherman to a slower pace of life. There is a reason the pursuit is called fishing and not catching. It is a reminder that these waters are an elusive force that requires cooperation, both lending and testing patience.

My children have a great love of fishing, and it provides poignant teaching moments. Fishing requires a tremendous amount of restraint and observation for success. Clumsily and carelessly making noise will only lead to frustration and an unsuccessful endeavor. With the triumph of each freshly caught fish, I get to highlight each one's unique texture and flavor as we all marvel at the variety of God's creation.

As the turbulent waters shape land, they simultaneously create the environment that gives life to the delight that is seafood. This harmony of a life at sea reminds us that patience and cooperation with such a powerful, overwhelming force are rewarded, and bear marvelous fruit.

relegated to our youth. Love asks us to recreate, to re-enliven, to redeem, and to renew. We want to be who we were then with what we know now.

Maybe the sea brings out of us an analogous form of who we want to be—unconsumed by the weight of our past, confident in where God has us now. We long to return to her like we long for the zeal of a first love. The waves prompt us to be playful, ageless, weightless. The sea reaches back to old tales and times and into some future horizon beyond which we cannot know. It is inexhaustible.

Recreate

A dear priest I have known for years is, at eighty-three years of age, one of the most youthful people I know. He drives all over multiple counties each day to provide spiritual direction and the sacraments, to give meditations, to lead retreats, and on and on, day after day. He is a world-class hiker and a fast mover, often bumping and bruising himself along the way. But he will stop to spend several minutes marveling at a cat or laughing at the eager amiability of a puppy. He is wise with an unrelenting sense of joy and mission overflowing from decades of committed prayer and a focus to strengthen his interior life. He is childlike—not in spite of all of that but because of it. Love of God does that to us.

Kreeft speaks to this sort of glimpse outside of time into eternity. "How can we pinpoint the power of the sea over our hearts? It's not just swimming that we love. It's easier to swim in a pool or in a lake than in the sea. Look at all the people who come to the sea but *don't* swim in it. Just knowing it's there, just being near it, is their satisfaction. Most visitors to the Alps are

not mountain climbers or skiers either. Just seeing her face is enough. It's a Beatific Vision. It's love."

A summer day at the beach is a shorthand for bliss for good reason. Music, poetry, films, and even the branding of California offer the promise or provide a reminder of the allure of the beach. The smell of suntan lotion, memories of bare feet scampering over hot dunes, the splash of a first bracingly cold wave, the sensation of sand on sticky skin, the early sunburn that softens into a tan, the sounds of open-air music, chatter, children, gulls, and the rhythm of the waves. It is a promised land contained in a postcard whispering to us in our office cubicle during the dead of a hard winter.

We don't leave the magic of the sea behind as we grow up and grow old, as though she were merely a childish activity. We sense that she is more significant than that. Tiring of the sea is not a common problem. The human capacity to watch waves roll in and out without losing interest is telling. "One of the surfer's best rules is never, never, never turn your back on the sea. She's big," says Kreeft. She commands our attention, and we sense that we have to contend with her. We want recreation because we want to be made new, and somehow this drive calls us out of a life of simple safety or utility and into a great adventure. It is not simply that we want to play but that we want to live.

CHAPTER 5

Water and Home

There is a wild unpredictability to the sea. Water is formless, primordial, and a signifier of change and chaos. And though we live life primarily with the surety of order and stability on land, still we desire that dynamism of the unknowable to vivify a life lived on solid ground.

A life of sheer order would not have growth. We need something to navigate: a suffering or an unexpected encounter jolting us out of our routine. We need what we do not know to come shake us, enliven us, pull us out of our facts and locked doors. In short, we need the grand adventure that comes from having something to revere and conform our lives to. The sense of smallness we feel in the face of the sea is important.

This dynamism of land and sea that so compels us is something of the essence of love itself. Love is both small and expansive. It is stable and wild, fatherly and motherly. It is the marriage of all these elements that expresses the richness of God's love and points us to him.

It is a cliché to dream of owning a beach house, and the dream is relatively out of reach for most. But what we want is to be near this life force, which explains in part why cities like Sydney and Hong Kong, Honolulu and Los Angeles, London and New York, Venice and Amsterdam, Lisbon and Istanbul, Mumbai and Manilla are crowded and bustling (and expensive).

———————

"When anxious, uneasy and bad thoughts come,
I go to the sea, and the sea drowns them out with its
great wide sounds, cleanses me with its noise, and imposes a
rhythm upon everything in me that is bewildered and confused."

—RAINER MARIA RILKE

———————

Bodies of water have always been a backdrop in my parents' life together, even predating that life. Born in the Philippines and having lived all over Europe, my mom dreamt one night of the famous Monet painting of a Japanese bridge over a pond with water lilies. She stood on one side of the bridge, and on the other was a man with dark hair and hazel eyes. The next morning, her mother told her they were moving to the States to live in San Francisco. Some months after their move, a new friend introduced her to my father at a party, and she instantly recognized him from her dream. On their first date, he took her to the beach and told her he would like to marry her.

They established their family in the Bay Area and would frequent the chilly San Francisco coastline, dreaming that someone with an oceanfront property would offer their house to them. "You're just the nice young couple that I want to pass my home to!" the stranger would announce in their fantasy. Of course, the fantasy remained just that, and within a few years, they had moved inland to California's Central Valley. The area never sat well with them. It aggravated his allergies, and she missed San Francisco's bracing cold, foghorns, and museums.

"Mary is the sea that no one exhausts;
the more one draws from it,
the more he finds."

—FRENCH KNIGHT

Nonetheless, they settled in. While I was a small child, my mom graduated from nursing school and began working. She promptly traded in her first paycheck for a family trip to the ocean. Many Christmases were spent in San Francisco, and summers found us traveling to various beach locales where we would cram into a hotel room and make sandwiches to enjoy by the sea.

After thirty years living in the valley, they were finally able to move near my family in a small California beach town. Today, she cares for him in his advanced state, and they enjoy the sea in a limited way—as a beautiful vista on drives to doctor appointments up the coast. The dreams of life become smaller and quieter than we might think early on when the questions of our lives have not yet been answered.

Still, they can't help but reminisce. Their devotion to one another is made and remade through the revisiting of that painting in her dream. They retell it to relive it and confirm to one another that, despite the oceans once separating them, their love was somehow preordained and there are no more questions. Their longing for that home at the sea was satiated in the life and in the

Bringing the Sea Inside

As my future husband and I knelt down shortly before Sunday Mass began at Notre Dame Cathedral in Paris, he whispered to me that life-changing question that is so often accompanied by a shiny ring held in a shaking, sweaty hand.

We were living in Rome at the time, so our first thought was to get married in Italy. But after realizing that most of our closest relatives wouldn't be able to make the trip, we changed our minds and moved it to the Oregon coast—to Astoria, the estuary where the Columbia River kisses the Pacific. Lewis and Clark spent a miserably wet winter there in the early nineteenth century before making their way back across the country. Our March wedding had a splash of unseasonably warm weather, then dark brooding clouds, followed by wind and rain. The day after our wedding, it snowed.

The wedding was at The Star of the Sea Catholic Church, with the reception at an old but newly renovated cannery—complete with exposed wooden beams and perched on pilings over the water in an effort to be as close as possible to receive the latest catch.

The mouth of the Columbia is a dangerous route with mighty and deep currents threatening ships piled high with mismatched shipping containers. The memory of watching these enormous ships navigate the treacherous waters was imprinted in my mind throughout the days spent there for the wedding.

I recently purchased a print that now hangs in my kitchen of a single shipping tanker with brightly-colored containers stacked like Legos sailing among wavy blue lines. It immediately takes me back to those formative days when friends from near and far, young and old, came to witness our wedding. It reminds me of those who are no longer with us and those who were just babies and now in their teens. And it reminds me of that special place where my husband and I, surrounded by rough waters and extreme weather, embarked on our life together, fortified by grace and with a new confidence and peace for whatever might lie ahead.

home they made with and in each other. But it is ultimately the promise of our eternal home that sits inside all of our longings in this life.

Author Thomas Howard wrote of this radical and true restoration offered to us by God:

> Behold I make all things new. Behold I do what cannot be done. I restore the years that the locusts and worms have eaten. I restore the years which you have drooped away upon your crutches and in your wheelchair. I restore the symphonies and operas which your deaf ears have never heard and the snowy massif your eyes have never seen and the freedom lost to you through plunder and the identity lost to you because of calumny and the failure of justice. And I restore the good which your own foolish mistakes have cheated you of. And I bring you to the love of which all other loves speak, the love which is joy and beauty, and which you have sought in a thousand streets, and for which you have wept and clawed your pillow.

Stella Maris

While studying abroad in southern France, I recall entering a small, darkened stone church somewhere off the beaten path, where the walls were packed with votive offerings: crutches, eyeglasses, painted pictures, small trinkets made to look like arms or legs or hearts, all offered as thanksgiving for an answered prayer. I'd never seen anything like it before. They were often old and dusty, thrown together without thoughtful placement, but their voices

still spoke through the ages that here in *this* place, Jesus and his mother had done something wonderful for someone. I saw them in other churches too. Those closer to the Mediterranean Sea often had pictures of boats, or oars, or a stormy sea. Votive offerings certainly aren't exclusive to Provence and can be found in all kinds of European churches, as well as in the Americas. One such church dating back to 1771 is Our Lady of Good Help in Old Montreal, Canada, which became a site of pilgrimage for sailors as they traveled to and from the New World. To this day, little wooden boats are still displayed, offered as petition or thanksgiving for safe travels upon the sea.

Our Lady's name has long been associated with water—with springs, as an aqueduct of grace, as a port to come home to. Stella Maris, or "Star of the Sea," is one of her oldest titles.

St. Jerome, in the fifth century, is often attributed with giving Mary this title for his translation of her name. It is difficult to know exactly for how many centuries it has passed the lips of those threated by the sea. The title was endorsed by theologians as well as simple folk who found a protectress and a guide in our Lady. So popular was the title and so prompt her aid that even the North Star was referred to as *Stella Maris*. She was the spiritual GPS, and prayers offered to her could be encapsulated in one simple phrase: *guide me home.*

St. Bernard of Clairvaux, a twelfth-century Burgundian abbot of the Cistercian Order, is perhaps best known for promoting our Lady's work. Of her, he wrote, "She is that glorious star lighting the way across this vast ocean of life, glowing with merits, guiding by example." He also recommended her aid well beyond natural trials to all sinners ensnared in temptation or moral struggles: "If the winds of temptation arise; If you are driven upon the rocks of tribulation look to the star, call on Mary; If you are tossed upon the waves of pride, of ambition, of envy, of rivalry, look to the star, call on Mary. Should anger, or avarice, or fleshly desire violently assail the frail vessel of your soul, look at the star, call upon Mary."

Later, St. Thomas Aquinas wrote succinctly, "Mary means Star of the Sea, for as mariners are guided to port by the ocean star, so Christians attain to glory through Mary's maternal intercession."

Such lofty language might not have stuck on a popular level if there hadn't been story after story of our Lady's aid for those in dire straits. Testimonies of Mary's help abound: fog suddenly clearing, storms calmed, sailors saved from drowning, winds picking up to fill a sail, and all sorts of other shifts in wind, water, and temperature, from the mundane to the miraculous.

A rich and beautiful picture of our Lady's ardent efforts is on display in Dante's *Divine Comedy*. In his epic voyage from hell, via purgatory, and finally into heaven, Dante is guided into a dark wood because of his mortal sin

and is transformed into a godly man who beheld the brightness of holiness captured in the heavens and the stars. But the stars, which shine brightly and prominently throughout the trilogy, may have more meaning than merely luminous celestial bodies. One scholar, Sheila J. Nayar, writes, "I propose that Mary as the Star of the Sea is alluded to, is called upon—is continuously *present* throughout the poem—serving as a sort of echo chamber, even as a kind of all-encompassing womb; and this is accomplished through Dante's frequent referencing of the stars, of seas, and of the bearing both these have on any nautical traveler." Mary is the protective and gentle mother who initiated Dante's journey and dispatched his guides, first Beatrice who then enlists

Jewel of the Sea

Beautiful treasures hidden in the depths of the sea are inaccessible to most human beings without great effort. Pearls are the quintessential jewels of the sea. Though clams and mussels can produce pearls as well, they are more often found in, and associated with, oysters. But that doesn't mean they are common to oysters. In fact, most oysters do not have pearls.

A pearl is a result of the entrance of an irritant into the shell of the oyster. The oyster's lining material envelopes the irritant in order to protect the interior anatomy of the mollusk. Eventually, that material surrounding the irritant becomes a pearl.

Not all pearls evolve into the perfectly white luminous orbs that the name tends to evoke in our imaginations. Color and shape may vary, and not all will be considered precious. But all begin with a wound and are formed and shaped and in some cases made beautiful and precious in response.

Virgil, to help him find his way home, even without his asking. Philosopher Ralph McInerny said, "The Blessed Virgin Mary is the key to Dante."

St. Bernard of Clairvaux captures some of the fervor felt by theologian and folk alike when it came to Our Lady, Star of the Sea, offering contem-

---

"Who more than Mary could be a star of hope for us?
With her 'yes' she opened the door of our world
to God himself; she became the living Ark of
the Covenant, in whom God took flesh, became one
of us, and pitched his tent among us (cf. John 1:14)."

–POPE BENEDICT XVI

---

porary readers a shorthand as to why Dante and his contemporaries would have immediately understood that the stars where symbols of Mary. "She is therefore that glorious star . . . whose ray illumines the entire earth, whose splendor shines out conspicuously in heaven and reaches even unto hell. . . . She, I say, is that resplendent and radiant star, placed as a necessary beacon above life's great and spacious sea."

In the poem, our Lady's first introduction begins in the *Inferno*—though not directly by name, because her name (like Jesus's) is too holy to be spoken there. "There is a gentle lady in heaven who weeps at this distress"

(*Inferno*, 2.94–95). The same description could be used with our Lady at La Salette, weeping for her children who have fallen into sin.

One could downplay the connection to our Lady and the *Comedy*, but ample evidence of Dante's deep affection for the stars and what they symbolize is on display as he ends every book with the word *stars*:

> He first and I behind, we climbed so high
> That through a small round opening I saw
> Some of the turning beauties of the sky.
> And we came out to see, once more, the stars. (*Inferno* 34.136–139)

> From its most holy waters I returned
> And remade as a new young plant appears
> Renewed in every newly springing frond,
> Pure, and in time for mounting to the stars. (*Purgatorio* 33. 142–145)

> Here ceased the powers of my high fantasy.
> Already were all my will and my desires
> turned – as a wheel in equal balance – by
> The Love that moves the sun and the other stars. (*Paradiso* 33.142–145)

More than dazzling props in his poem, Dante subtly reveals how our Lady accompanies him on this journey, lighting his way, guiding him, tending to him like a good mother.

Upon his arrival in paradise, the poet's language becomes more allegorical to accommodate that which is ineffable, but Dante clearly speaks of our Lady as a star and as the Queen of Heaven:

The sound of that sweet flower's name,
the one I pray to night and day,
drew all my soul into the vision of that flame of flames;
and when both of my eyes revealed to me
how rich and glorious was that living star
that reigns in Heaven, as it had reigned on Earth,
down from Heaven's height there came
a flaming torch shaped in a ring, as if it were a crown,
that spun around the glory of her light. (*Paradiso* 23.88–96)

Far from being merely a travel guide for the curious (especially about hell), Dante's poem is a map for safely navigating us to our true home, with the stars illuminating the way.

DeAnn Malcolm

I buttoned my dress and took a deep breath, but not too deep. *I can't pop a button*, I thought, pregnant with our eighth child. *I can do this. I can manage this many children, one with a mystery illness. Right, God?*

At the wedding, I learned a new Marian title: Stella Maris. I also realized, as I danced with the bride's parents and *not* the bridal party, that I was old; old *and* pregnant.

The next day, we headed to the beach for our annual vacation. It is the place where my soul finds rest. The sea and he who parts it, calms it, and walks upon it have always been sources of wonder, peace, and connection for me and my family. As we drove, I thought about Stella Maris.

After unpacking, food shopping, dinner, baths, and bed for the kids, I finally had a moment to put my toes in the sand. The stress of another pregnancy weighed heavily upon me. After several miscarriages, I was grateful and open to this life but felt woefully unprepared. Stella Maris floated into my mind. "Star of the Sea." Comforter of those who are lost. She shows them the way. I looked at the night sky and spotted a very bright star.

"You can do this," she gently whispered into my heart.

"Yes, Mother Mary; with your help, I can do this."

Eight months later, we joyfully welcomed Stella Marie.

Similitude

An important and vital role in Dante's salvation is played by the beautiful and virtuous Beatrice. Before there was any *Divine Comedy*, she was Dante's muse to whom he devoted his heart; it was her beauty and goodness that sent him on his quest. His interest started with mere carnal passion, and then, tragically, she died, which sent Dante to the depths of despair and a dissolute life. His contact with women who lacked virtue escalated his devotion to Beatrice. As Ralph McInerny says, "His love for Beatrice finally emerges in his great poem as the means of his salvation."

In *The Divine Comedy*, Dante writes her in as his guide after Virgil, the symbol of reason, leads him through hell and most of purgatory. Beatrice

takes over as his guide as a symbol of love, which is required for true salvation beyond mere reason. She is so radiant that, at times, it is difficult for Dante to look at her. She and all of paradise are dazzling beyond comprehension. Beatrice serves Dante both as a physical guide through heaven but also as a kind of mediator that helps him see beauty and goodness at a previously unknown level. She leads him, by way of her similarity to the Queen of Heaven, to a deep and true devotion to our Lady. His love for Beatrice, and her goodness, is the springboard to deeper and fuller love. And Mary's love and goodness always point to her Son, the one who can finally bring peace to Dante's heart.

The similitude between Beatrice and our Lady is not insignificant. As the late Norbertine priest Fr. Cadoc Leighton explained, "Closeness, in the spiritual realm, . . . is similitude." He continues, "The Second Person of the Blessed Trinity has become one *like us*, so that we can become *like Him*. In [Mary's] life we see the process of our redemption revealed, because we see her similitude to her Son. We cannot actually contemplate Mary *without* contemplating Jesus at the same time." Fr. Leighton emphasizes that similitude is a vital element in Christianity because it offers us a model to follow, a way to be educated, and a path to salvation. Mary's similitude to Jesus, he adds, "is the revelation of what the process of salvation *is*, up close."

But what if someone has never encountered Mary as a mother? We can see how vital the Beatrices of the world are, that she and women like her can offer a human model of feminine virtue and beauty. They can help elevate those who are searching for something or someone to help bring rest to their hearts, even if they may not know it. We are called to be like Beatrice, to guide others to God through our similitude to him and his mother.

Afterword

There is something about life on the sea that Christians have always been called to mimic. It is a recognition that this world isn't our true home, that it is passing and transitory, that our treasure ought not to be stored up here but in the world beyond.

Sailors know this deep in their bones. There is order on a ship because seafarers must be prepared for the unexpected. There can frequently be a sense of high alert, of preparing for the worst as the unknown lurks, perhaps as close as the other side of the next wave.

Often, on land, we can be lulled into thinking everything is steady and permanent and will go on like this forever. And yet, as St. Anselm of Canterbury said, "Disasters teach us humility." That is the lesson of the sea, that we are preciously small compared to its vast force. But we also know that even in our smallness, we are still precious in the eyes of God.

There is a story about the return of Christopher Columbus and his crew to Spain after they discovered the New World. A storm came upon them, and in their fear, they prayed to our Lady for her intercession to end the storm. When the storm continued, they cast lots to see who among them would, if they survived, make a barefoot pilgrimage to Our Lady of Guadalupe deep in the heart of Spain (the first Our Lady of Guadalupe before she appeared in Mexico in 1531). When still the storm raged on and they began to fear that they would never make it home, they agreed that they would *all* make this pilgrimage to our Lady's shrine.

And with that, the storm ended and the waters grew calm.

Upon their arrival, after being greeted with a hero's welcome, Columbus and the other sailors, true to their promise, promptly made the arduous pilgrimage on foot to honor our Lady with their lives and love.

We know this world isn't our ultimate home. We know we are wayfarers, pilgrims, sailors. But God has provided us with the necessary ship and star to help us on our journey. We can travel like the saints with confidence and trust and take the advice offered by St. Jane de Chantal: "Today, when any thoughts or worries come to mind, send them out into the ocean of God's love that surrounds you and lose them there. If any feelings come into your heart—grief, fear, even joy or longing, send those out into the ocean of God's love. Finally, send your whole self, like a drop, into God. There is no past no future, here or there. There is only the infinite ocean of God."

Our Lady, Star of the Sea, guide us home!

Bibliography

Cadoc D. Leighton. "A Retreat on The Immaculate Conception of the Blessed Virgin Mary." Leominster, Herefordshire: Gracewing, 2021.

Dante. *Paradise, Purgatory, Inferno*. Translated by Anthony Esolen. New York: Modern Library Classics, 2004.

Homer. *The Odyssey*. Revised translation of E. V. Rieu. New York: Penguin Classics, 1946.

Peter Kreeft. *The Sea Within*. South Bend, Indiana: St. Augustine's Press, 2006.

Peter Kreeft. "The Sea Within." Black Friars Film. YouTube. 2016. https://www.youtube.com/watch?v=qRbWQFvIi44.

Ralph McInerny. "Dante and the Blessed Virgin." Jacques Maritain Center, University of Notre Dame, 2021. https://maritain.nd.edu/jmc/etext/DBVM.htm.

Sheila J. Nayar. "Dante's Star of the Sea: The Narrative Constellation of Mary in the Divine Comedy." *Literature and Theology* 33.1 (2019).

St. Albert the Great. *The Valiant Woman*. Translated by Benedict M. Ashley and Dominic M. Hotlz. Chicago: New Priory Press, 2013. Kindle Edition.

CARRIE GRESS (right) is a Fellow at The Ethics and Public Policy Center and a Scholar at The Institute for Human Ecology at Catholic University of America. She is a prolific writer and author of several books, including *The Marian Option*, *The Anti-Mary Exposed*, and *Theology of Home*. She and her husband, and five children, live in Virginia. She is also the editor of the online Catholic women's magazine, TheologyofHome.com.

NOELLE MERING (left) is a Fellow at the Washington DC-based think tank the Ethics and Public Policy Center. She is the author of *Awake, Not Woke* and *Theology of Home* and editor for TheologyofHome.com. She lives with her husband and six children in Southern California.

KIM BAILE (center) has been a lifestyle and commercial photographer for over 10 years, and has had the pleasure of documenting many of life's moments from newborns and families to seasonal campaigns for global brands. She and her husband, Mark, live in Southern California.